The Loch Ness Monster

The

LOCH NESS MONSTER

Lian
1995
CD

Elaine Landau

The Millbrook Press ❑ Brookfield, Connecticut
Mysteries of Science

Library of Congress Cataloging-in-Publication Data

Landau, Elaine.
The Loch Ness monster / by Elaine Landau.
p.   cm.—(Mysteries of Science)
Includes bibliographical references (p.   ) and index.
Summary: Introduces the folklore and reported sightings of the
unidentified creature known as the Loch Ness Monster and evaluates
the evidence for and against its existence.
ISBN 1-56294-347-2 (lib. bdg.)
1. Loch Ness monster—Juvenile literature.   [1. Loch Ness
monster.   2. Monsters.]   I. Title.   II. Series: Landau, Elaine.
Mysteries.
QL89.2.L6L36   1993
001.9'44—dc20   92-35145   CIP   AC

Published by The Millbrook Press
2 Old New Milford Road, Brookfield, Connecticut 06804

Contents

Chapter One
Something Strange in the Water 9

Chapter Two
The Search Begins 19

Chapter Three
The Hunt Continues 27

Glossary 44

Further Reading 45

Index 46

Cover illustration and design, and illustration on p. 8
by Anne Canevari Green

Photos courtesy of: International Society of Cryptozoology:
pp. 10, 34, 40; National Audubon Society Collection/Photo
Researchers: p. 13; Giraudon/Art Resource: p. 14; Bettmann
Archive: pp. 15, 29; *Inverness Courier:* p. 17 (photo by Ken
Macpherson); British Tourist Authority: pp. 20, 21; UPI/
Bettmann: pp. 23, 36; New York Public Library Picture
Collection: p. 24; AP/Wide World Photos: pp. 30, 39, 42;
Richard Raynor, La Pergola, Kilmuir: p. 33; © Academy
of Applied Science, RHR, 1972, 1975: p. 37.

For Grace Noyes McLaughry

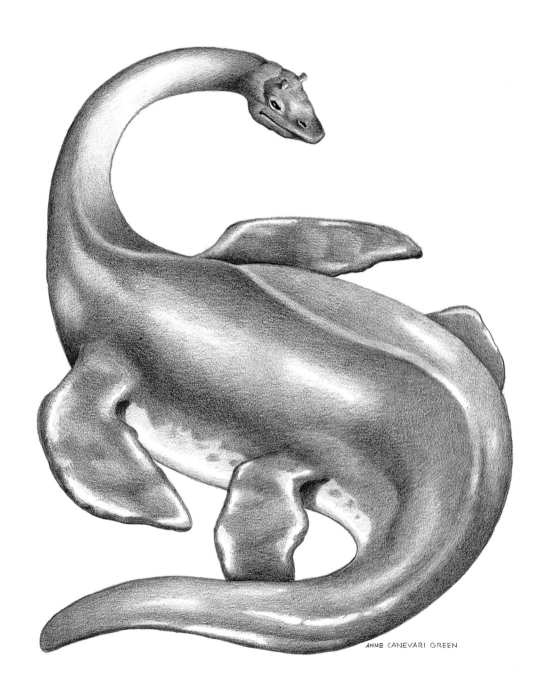

ANNE CANEVARI GREEN

Something Strange in the Water

Picture a large monster that lives in water.
Two short, stubby horns crown its narrow head.
Its long neck stretches out from its wide,
round body. Its curved back makes it look a
little like a big, upside-down boat.
Flippers on its sides and its powerful tail propel
it fast through the water.

Although it may sound unbelievable, many
people have said that they have seen this
creature. They say it dwells in Scotland—
a region of the United Kingdom, north of
England—in a lake called Loch Ness. (**Loch**
is the Scottish word for lake.) They call
this animal the Loch Ness Monster or Nessie.

*Conservationist Sir Peter Scott
painted this pair of Nessies based on
many eyewitness accounts.*

Despite the fact that people have sworn they have seen Nessie, others say that such an animal cannot possibly exist. If it does not exist, what can explain the sightings of something strange in the waters of Loch Ness? And if Nessie does exist, what is it and where did it come from?

Theories About Nessie ❏ Several theories attempt to explain what Nessie is and how it came to be. According to one, Nessie's origins lie at the end of a period of history called the **Ice Age** about 12,000 years ago. At that time, Scotland was buried under huge masses of ice called **glaciers.** These glaciers began to melt. Their water ran into the sea surrounding Scotland, causing it to rise.

Much of the land became flooded. This allowed creatures that lived in the sea to travel to these flooded land areas—called **fjords**—and live and reproduce in them. Some of these creatures may have been large and unusual animals that today we can only imagine as monsters.

About seven thousand years ago, the floods began to go down. Soon these fjords were no longer connected to the sea by water. Land surrounded them and they became lakes. In the process, some of these strange sea creatures may have found themselves trapped in the newly formed lakes.

Conditions in the lakes began to change. Their salty seawater was slowly replaced by fresh water from rain and from water feeding into them from streams. Some sea animals died out. But others adapted to their new environment and survived.

Is Nessie related to a giant, trapped sea monster of long ago? Some people think so. They have compared Nessie to **plesiosaurs**—a group of water-dwelling dinosaurs. Plesiosaurs had necks and bodies similar to the kind Nessie is said to have. Plesiosaurs were also fish-eaters, as Nessie is reported to be. Is Nessie a modern plesiosaur?

Scientists point out that plesiosaurs have been extinct for over 60 million years. Plesiosaurs, moreover, were **cold-blooded.** They received their heat from the surrounding environment. A plesiosaur could not possibly receive enough heat from Loch Ness's cold waters to survive. Plesiosaurs also breathed air. If Nessie were related to them, it would have to surface regularly for oxygen. But Nessie has not been seen regularly. Nessie would have to have changed greatly from the earlier plesiosaurs over the past 60 million years.

History of Sightings ❑ It has been argued that throughout history people have encountered unusual water-dwelling creatures. Ancient stone carvings showing such beasts have been found in Scotland and elsewhere. Ships belonging to the **Vikings**—northern European pirates of the eighth, ninth, and tenth centuries—were shaped to look like sea serpents. Could these ships have been modeled after Nessie's ancestors?

People have reported seeing giant water creatures in the area around Loch Ness for hundreds of years. In A.D. 565, Saint Columba—a priest—is said to have observed a giant water beast in the River Ness, which is part of Loch Ness.

There have been many stories and folktales like Columba's. At first, the large swimming beasts in these stories were said to be evil. Some even thought the Devil himself lurked below the loch's surface. As a result, local people often hesitated to admit they had seen anything strange. The giant water creatures were not often discussed outside the small communities surrounding Loch Ness.

Are the plesiosaurs shown in this painting Nessie's ancestors?

*Was Nessie the model for the long, curling design
of the Viking ship in this stone carving?*

But as time passed, admitting contact with these creatures must have become less threatening. Tales of "water
beasts," as they were often called, grew more common. Many
people who lived near Loch Ness recalled hearing stories in
childhood of these massive swimmers.

Hundreds of years ago, people depicted strange water monsters in engravings like this one. Were their depictions based on Nessie sightings?

Beginning of World Fame ❑ During the 1870s, a Loch Ness–area man named Donald Mackenzie reported seeing a creature in Loch Ness. Mackenzie said he was walking along the loch when he spotted something that looked like an "upturned" boat floating in the water. Moments later he realized that what he had seen was alive. The creature then bolted off through the water.

Although Mackenzie described what he saw to his friends and neighbors, the story did not receive very much attention. A dozen or so sightings similar to Mackenzie's followed. They were also ignored.

In fact, neither the public nor scientists became interested in the matter until the 1930s. At that time, a construction project began to widen a road running directly past Loch Ness. This road offered travelers good views of some 20 miles (32 kilometers) of the loch and, supposedly, of Nessie.

One of the most important sightings of this period was reported by a Loch Ness–area couple, Mr. and Mrs. John Mackay. On a March afternoon in 1933, the Mackays were driving along the loch. Suddenly, Mrs. Mackay said she saw "an enormous black body" rise out of the water. By the time her husband stopped the car, it was gone.

A friend of the Mackays told the story to a man named Alex Campbell who wrote for a local newspaper called the *Inverness Courier*. Campbell wrote an account of the Mackays' experience based on what he had heard. When Campbell gave the account to the paper, its editor remarked: "Well, if it's as

A 1933 article in the Inverness Courier *made public an account of the Mackays' monster sighting.*

big as Campbell says it is, we can't just call it a creature. It must be a real monster." So the creature received the name Loch Ness Monster.

On May 2, 1933, the *Inverness Courier* published Campbell's story. It described the Mackays' sighting in dramatic detail. It reported that the creature had a body "resembling that of a whale." According to Campbell's story, the monster was so large that when it dove down it sent water in the lake "cascading and churning like a simmering cauldron. . . . Taking the final plunge, [it] sent out waves that were big enough to have been caused by a passing steamer." The local public was stunned and fascinated by Campbell's account. Soon, other sightings of monsters were reported—many of which matched the Mackays'.

❏ ❏ ❏

As reports of sightings increased, so did questions about Nessie. Since the number of sightings had risen so sharply, people wondered whether there might be more than one monster. Did a family of Nessies live in the lake? Could these creatures be sensitive to sound? Would the rock blasting and loud noises associated with the road construction prompt them to begin surfacing more often?

These questions remained unanswered. But the attention focused on Nessie from 1933 to 1934 paved the way for the creature's international fame. Before long, reporters and tourists from around the world flocked to Scotland hoping to catch a glimpse of Nessie. Suddenly, everyone wanted to know if one or more monsters really lived in Loch Ness.

People who lived near the lake felt certain an unusual creature dwelled in its waters. These people would soon learn, however, that the rest of the world was not as ready to share their belief.

The Search Begins

The thought of finding a live water monster
was exciting. But Nessie-hunters soon
realized their task would not be easy.
Loch Ness measures 1 mile (1.6 kilometers)
wide and 24 miles (39 kilometers) long. It may
also be among the deepest lakes in Europe.
Much of the loch reaches a depth of 500 feet
(153 meters) or more, and in some spots goes
more than 800 feet (244 meters) down. Loch
Ness, in fact, is so big that if it were empty,
three times the number of men, women, and
children in the world could fit inside it.
Searching a lake that large for anything—
even a monster—was a difficult task.

Loch Ness under a sky of gathering gloom: The area's weather, often windy and rainy, hindered some monster-hunters.

These ruins of Urquhart Castle overlook
some of the deepest parts of Loch Ness, where
many said they have seen the monster.

Besides the loch's tremendous size, monster-searchers had to deal with its murky water. Tiny particles of decomposing plants—known as **peat**—float in the water, giving it a brown color. Even with the aid of special lighting, observers could not see more than a few feet through the water.

Early Expeditions ❑ Despite such problems, many Nessie-hunters came to the loch. People interested in Nessie funded early expeditions. In 1934, Sir Edward Mountain, a wealthy Englishman, hired twenty men to carefully watch the loch for ten hours a day. Each man had a camera and a pair of binoculars. After twenty-five weeks, the team reported about twenty sightings of what they believed was Nessie. The observers photographed five of the sightings. But a careful examination of the photos later revealed that at least four were of ordinary objects in the water, or of waves that had been made by boats.

A second expedition followed Mountain's and lasted for several weeks. This time observers filmed what they had seen in the water. The film appeared to show a large animal splashing in the loch. But it was impossible to prove that this creature was Nessie and not some other, more ordinary type of animal—or even a large school of fish.

Yet reports of new sightings continued to fill Scottish newspapers. Some seemed more believable than others. According to one account, a monster family including two baby monsters lived in the lake.

False Sightings ❑ Some people saw the increased interest in Nessie during the 1930s as an opportunity to deliberately fool the public. A group of Boy Scouts built a monster out of canvas and wood and floated it on the lake. Some took the fake creature for Nessie. On another occasion, a large

*Many believed that the dark shape in the lower
right corner of this photo from the Mountain
expedition was Nessie moving underwater.*

*A star is born: This faked
photo shows Nessie hamming
it up for a video camera.
The side of the boat reads:
Loch Ness Boat Rentals.*

greenish-brown foot appeared in the lake. Although at first it was thought to belong to Nessie, it turned out to be an ordinary crocodile's foot put there as a trick.

A London newspaper, *The Daily Mail*, hired a hunter noted for success in tracking down large creatures in the wild to find Nessie. The hunter did spot some footprints he thought could belong to a large creature. But these turned out to be the work of pranksters who created them with a stuffed hippopotamus foot.

While some dreamed up stunts such as these to fool the public, others hoped to become rich or famous by pretending to have seen Nessie. Some people even charged that the Loch Ness Monster was the result of a story made up to benefit Scotland's tourist trade. Tourists rarely visited Scotland during winter months due to the area's cold weather. Yet during the Christmas season of 1933, hotels surrounding Loch Ness were filled with tourists anxious to catch a glimpse of Nessie. Local businesses boomed. One inn even added a new wing to meet the growing demand for rooms.

Stories surfaced that a group of local businessmen had dreamed up Nessie one night while drinking at a local bar. According to these stories, the businessmen thought that news of a **prehistoric** water monster might catch the public's attention and bring visitors to Scotland.

In addition to the possibility of such dishonest activities, a number of honest mistakes put Nessie-hunting in a negative light. According to local residents, while the 1930s road construction around the lake made for increased Nessie sightings, it also made for some embarrassing moments. At one point during construction, empty barrels that had been filled with tar for the road were left to float on the loch. Some people mistook these for bumps in Nessie's back.

Thorough investigations of the 1930s sightings also revealed that shadows on the lake's water from flying ducks and ripples from gusts of wind had been mistaken for Nessie. Partially sunken tree trunks, floating logs, and clumps of dead plants were thought to be the monster as well.

No matter how sincere they were, Nessie-spotters often only caught glimpses of what they believed was the creature. Incidents such as these left room for doubt about Nessie's existence.

The Hunt Continues

Due to the lack of convincing evidence of Nessie's existence, few thorough scientific investigations of the Loch Ness Monster were conducted until the 1960s. Scientists pointed out that even though there had been many Nessie sightings during the 1930s, people who reported them were untrained in biology and other sciences. As a result, scientists thought, these people might have believed they were seeing a monster when they were actually seeing other types of animals.

In 1961, Maurice Burton, a British scientist who studied mammals, proposed that sightings of Nessie had actually been sightings of a species of large, long-neck otters that he thought might live in the lake. Burton pointed out that otters living in cold northern climates such as Scotland's often reached up to 6 and even 8 feet (1.8 and 2.5 meters) in length. According to Burton, many Nessie observers might have easily mistaken these giant otters for monsters. Burton's theory, however, remained unproven.

Scientists during the 1960s also dismissed Nessie photographs. Even the best shots of the "monster" drew suspicion. A London surgeon named R. Kenneth Wilson took in 1934 what was seemingly one of the clearest and most detailed photographs of Nessie ever. The photo, which was published on April 21 in London's *Daily Mail* newspaper, received a great deal of fascinated attention. Wilson, however, never actually claimed he had photographed the Loch Ness Monster. He merely said he had snapped a picture of something in the loch. According to some, R. Kenneth Wilson himself even hinted that the photo was taken as a prank on April Fool's Day. In 1994, it was revealed that the photograph was in fact a fake.

New Technology ❑ While the question of the monster's existence persisted, Nessie enthusiasts remained hopeful that one day they would be proven right. Their hopes were raised in the early 1960s when the Loch Ness Investigation Bureau

*Have people mistaken large otters like
the one in this engraving for Nessie?*

(LNIB) was established. This organization's goal was to conduct orderly, scientific team-searches for Nessie.

LNIB used a variety of methods to achieve this goal. Its members photographed the lake's surface and patrolled its depths with submarines. They also sent sound waves through the water. If there were a large object in the water, these sound waves would bounce off the object. People monitoring the waves could then tell how big the object was. This method of searching for things underwater is called **sonar.**

In addition to sonar, LNIB researchers used special sound equipment—called **hydrophones**—to "listen" for Nessie. Many thought that a creature as big as Nessie might make unusual noises, as whales do. But the researchers were not able to pick up any unusual animal sounds.

If they could not reach Nessie through sound, LNIB members thought, perhaps they could reach it through snacks. Researchers tried to coax Nessie to the surface by leaving various foods floating on the water. In case the monster appeared, one LNIB member, Roy P. Mackal of the University of Chicago, had a special gun that could shoot darts into the animal and bring back samples of its skin. These guns were attached to the submarines.

R. Kenneth Wilson's famous photo, revealed in 1994 as a fake.

LNIB's efforts succeeded in part. Sonar tests showed that several large, moving objects existed in the loch. In addition, LNIB learned that great numbers of fish lived in the lake— perhaps even enough to feed a huge creature like Nessie. Researchers using sonar to map the lake's terrain discovered underwater slopes with several large openings that could serve as hiding places for Nessie.

By the end of the 1960s, LNIB had also collected some exciting film footage. Several bits of film suggested that a large, unidentified, fish-eating animal lived in the loch. One piece of film showed a school of salmon fleeing from a large creature that LNIB members believed to be Nessie.

❏ ❏ ❏

But LNIB encountered numerous problems and dead ends as well. It needed more money and staff to continue its work. Both, however, became increasingly difficult to find. At the time of LNIB's founding, interest in the Loch Ness Monster was widespread. The organization's membership grew to nearly a thousand people. But many of these members were from outside Scotland. As a result, most could not participate in the organization's activities for long periods of time. Lack of money and full-time workers finally forced the organization to shut down by the early 1970s.

New Pictures of Nessie ❏ Meanwhile, people not connected with LNIB had also carried on the hunt for Nessie. In the

LNIB researcher Richard Raynor captured on film this streak in the water. Many believed it was Nessie, swimming close to the surface at top speed.

*Prepared to meet the monster: Timothy Dinsdale
with his cameras at Loch Ness.*

spring of 1960, Timothy Dinsdale, a British engineer, traveled to Loch Ness in search of the monster. During a six-day watch on the loch, Dinsdale obtained what many believed was the best movie footage of Nessie ever taken. His film showed a huge creature moving—according to those who analyzed the film—at least 10 miles (16 kilometers) per hour.

Within months, Dinsdale's film was being shown on television. This encouraged students from two of Britain's top universities—Oxford and Cambridge—to begin their own

Nessie hunts. When photo analysts from Britain's Royal Air Force studied Dinsdale's film, they concluded that he had photographed a living creature about 5 feet wide (152 centimeters) and 6 feet long (183 centimeters). Could the creature be Nessie?

In 1970 the Academy of Applied Science in Concord, New Hampshire, joined the search. Under the direction of Robert Rines, in 1972 the group took two underwater photographs of what was believed to be Nessie's flipper. The diamond-shaped flipper in the photos was calculated to be 4 feet (122 centimeters) wide by an amazing 8 feet long (244 centimeters). In 1975 the group took another series of photos showing a front view of Nessie. One picture was thought to be a close-up of the monster's horned head. Another showed what some think is the creature's long neck and massive body.

Did these photographs finally prove Nessie's existence? Some Nessie believers thought so. Scientists at the British Museum in London, however, criticized the photos severely. They believed the images in the photos had been changed through the use of computers. Others said that the pictures were still not clear enough to be taken as hard evidence.

The public often grew impatient over such disagreements. At one point there was even a demand to drain the lake and settle the matter once and for all. This would, however, be nearly impossible. Even if the world's largest water pumps were used, it would take years to complete the task. And where could Loch Ness's 263 billion cubic feet (7.4 billion cubic meters) of water be stored?

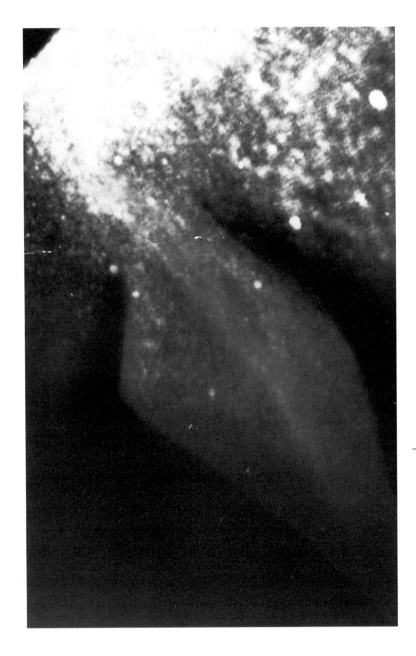

Are these Academy of Applied Science photos glimpses of Nessie's flipper . . .

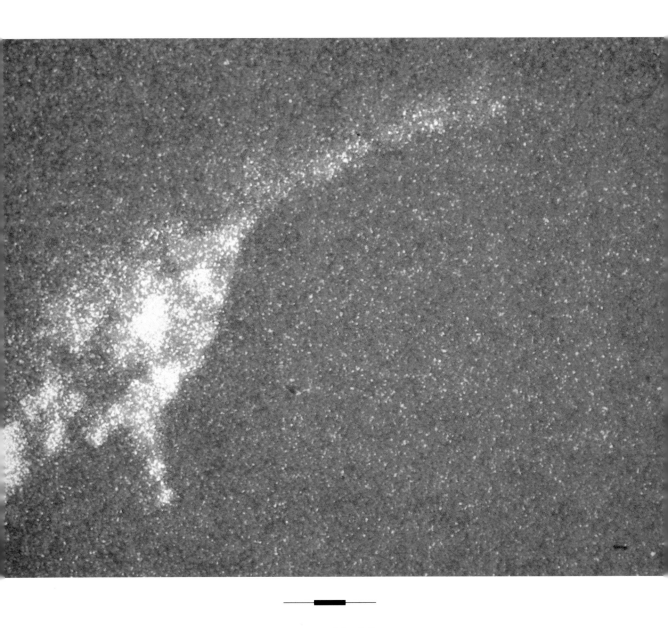

. . . and body?

The hunt for Nessie continued in more conventional ways. But during the late 1970s and 1980s, equipment and methods used in the search became increasingly advanced. The U.S. Navy loaned the Academy of Applied Science some of its latest underwater scanning equipment. During the 1980s the Academy also began training dolphins to carry cameras while swimming in the lake in the hope of catching a definitive photo of the monster.

While organizations and individuals continued to search for a monster in Loch Ness, reports of a similar monster in another Scottish lake, Loch Morar, began to surface. After investigating the reports, researchers pointed out that the lakes were very similar. Both have steep sides and are very deep. Like the people living near Loch Ness, Loch Morar-area residents also said that for many years they had heard stories from their ancestors of strange creatures living in the water.

In order to learn more about monster sightings in both lakes, Britain's Loch Ness and Morar Project was founded. Leaders of the Project—as it was called—did not trust much of the previous information that had been collected about

In 1983, American photographer Erik Beckjord snapped this picture of a boat (left) and a strange object (upper right) in the waters of Loch Ness.

Nessie. Too much of it, they believed, was based on eyewitness accounts. They demanded solid scientific evidence.

Important Sonar Findings ❏ Project leaders felt the best scientific work in searching for Nessie had been LNIB's sonar tests. They began building on these sonar tests throughout the 1980s. Project leaders also managed to attract researchers from various governments and university scientists to join them. This gave a new seriousness to the task of tracking down unusual creatures in both lakes.

Loch Morar: Is it the home of another Nessie?

In 1987 the Project concentrated its efforts on Loch Ness with an undertaking called Operation Deepscan. Twenty boats equipped with sonar units traveled up and down the lake. Something extremely important occurred during the operation. Scientists reported that sonar tests detected a living object believed to be larger than any animal known to live in a freshwater lake environment. Could it be Nessie—or some other type of large, unusual water creature?

Encouraged by the finding, the Loch Ness and Morar Project set up a full-time research station aboard a 34 foot (10.4 meters) boat at the center of Loch Ness. Scientists worked at the station trying to find more pieces to the Loch Ness Monster puzzle. They also broadened the scope of their work and began collecting as much information as possible about the loch's environment. They hope to find out exactly what types of large animals could survive in Loch Ness.

To write this book, I visited Loch Ness where I spoke with Adrian Shine, Director of the Loch Ness and Morar Project. When I asked him if he thought Nessie really existed, Shine replied: "People see strange things in Loch Ness. Sometimes we come up with strange sonar readings as well. We want to find out if the two are connected."

❏ ❏ ❏

In 1992 news of another water monster surfaced across the Atlantic from Scotland in Canada. Ogopogo, as the creature was called, was spotted by a television crew in a lake in the

Adrian Shine (left) stands on the deck
of an Operation Deepscan boat in another
attempt to solve the mystery of Nessie.

country's southwest region. One witness described the creature as "something that looked like a huge serpent."

Was Ogopogo Nessie's American cousin? Some **cryptozoologists**—scientists who study hidden or previously unknown animals—asserted that evidence strongly supported the possibility of a large marine animal in the area. That animal, they added, could be related to the creature said to dwell in Loch Ness. Some say the more we learn about Nessie, the closer we will come to finding out if others like it exist.

Perhaps future research will provide the answers. For now we can only continue to wonder whether or not there is something strange in the water of Loch Ness—the site of one of the world's continuing mysteries.

Glossary

cold-blooded—having a body temperature that adjusts to the temperature of the surrounding environment.

cryptozoologists—scientists who study hidden or previously unknown animals.

fjord—body of water usually found between cliffs or steep slopes.

glacier—large mass of ice moving slowly down a slope or spreading outward on land.

hydrophones—instruments used to listen to sounds transmitted through water.

Ice Age—period of the earth's history when large glaciers covered much of the land.

loch—Scottish word for lake.

peat—particles of decomposing plants in water.

plesiosaurs—species of water-dwelling dinosaurs.

prehistoric—existing in time before written history.

sonar—short for *so*und *n*avigation *a*nd *r*anging; a method of detecting objects underwater by sending out sound waves and measuring how long it takes them to return after striking objects.

Vikings—Northern European pirates of the eighth, ninth, and tenth centuries.

Further Reading

Abels, Harriette S. *The Loch Ness Monster*. New York: Crestwood House, 1987.

Berke, Sally. *Monster at Loch Ness*. Milwaukee: Raintree Steck-Vaughn, 1983.

Leen, Nina. *Rare and Unusual Animals*. New York: Henry Holt, 1981.

San Souci, Robert. *The Loch Ness Monster: Opposing Viewpoints*. San Diego: Greenhaven, 1989.

Selsam, Millicent E. *Sea Monsters of Long Ago*. New York: Four Winds, 1987.

Index

Page numbers in *italics* refer to illustrations.

Academy of Applied Science, Concord, New Hampshire, 35, 38

Beckjord, Erik, 38
British Museum, 35
Burton, Maurice, 28

Campbell, Alex, 16–17
Canada, 41, 43
Cold-blooded, 12
Columba, Saint, 12
Cryptozoologists, 43

Daily Mail, The, 25, 28
Dinsdale, Timothy, 34–35

Dolphins, 38

False sightings, 22, *24*, 25
Films, *33*, 34–35
Fish, 11, 32
Fjords, 11

Glaciers, 11

Hydrophones, 31

Ice Age, 11
Inverness Courier, 16, *17*

Loch, defined, 9
Loch Morar, 38, *40*
Loch Ness, 9, *20*
    drainage idea, 35

Loch Ness
  (*continued*)
    exploration of, 31–32, 38, 40–41,
      42
    road construction around, 16, 18,
      25–26
    size and depth of, 19
    water of, 12, 21
Loch Ness and Morar Project, 38, 40–
  41, 42
Loch Ness Investigation Bureau
  (LNIB), 28, 31–32, 40
Loch Ness Monster
    ancestors, 11–12, 13
    engraving of, 15
    false sightings, 22, 24, 25
    films, 33, 34–35
    painting of, 10
    photographs, 22, 23, 24, 28, 30, 35,
      36, 37, 39
    scientists and, 27–28, 31–32, 35,
      38, 40–41
    search for, 19, 21–22, 25
    sonar tests, 31, 32, 40, 41
    world fame, 16–18

Mackal, Roy P., 31
Mackay, Mr. and Mrs. John, 16, 17
Mackenzie, Donald, 16
Mountain, Sir Edward, 22

Nessie (*see* Loch Ness Monster)

Ogopogo, 41, 42
Operation Deepscan, 41, 42

Otters, 28, 29

Peat, 21
Photographs, 22, 23, 24, 28, 30, 35, 36,
  37, 39
Plesiosaurs, 11–12, 13
Prehistoric, 25

Raynor, Richard, 33
Rines, Robert, 35
River Ness, 12

Scientists, 12, 27–28, 31–32, 35, 38, 40–
  41
Scotland, 9, 11, 25 (*see also* Loch Ness;
  Loch Ness Monster)
Scott, Sir Peter, 10
Sea serpents, 12
Shine, Adrian, 41, 42
Ships, Viking, 12, 14
Sightings, 10, 12, 14, 16–18, 22, 26
Sonar, 31, 32, 40, 41
Submarines, 31

Tourists, 18, 25

U.S. Navy, 38
Urquhart Castle, 21

Vikings, 12

Whales, 31
Wilson, R. Kenneth, 28, 31

About the Author

Elaine Landau has written over fifty books
for young people. She received her bachelor's
degree from New York University in English and
journalism and her master's degree in library
and information science from Pratt Institute.

While researching this book, Ms. Landau
visited Loch Ness. She arrived in Scotland
firmly believing that the Loch Ness Monster
was nothing more than a myth. But by the
time she returned to the United States she
was no longer sure that this was so.